LIFE IN THE
US ARMY

by Carrie Myers

BrightPoint Press

San Diego, CA

BrightP◇int Press

© 2021 BrightPoint Press
an imprint of ReferencePoint Press, Inc.
Printed in the United States

For more information, contact:
BrightPoint Press
PO Box 27779
San Diego, CA 92198
www.BrightPointPress.com

LIBRARY OF CONGRESS CATALOGING-IN-PUBLICATION DATA

Names: Myers, Carrie, author.
Title: Life in the US Army / Carrie Myers.
Description: San Diego : ReferencePoint Press, 2021. | Series: Life in the military | Includes
    bibliographical references and index. | Audience: Grades 10-12
Identifiers: LCCN 2020002462 (print) | LCCN 2020002463 (eBook) | ISBN 9781682829714
    (hardcover) | ISBN 9781682829721 (eBook)
Subjects: LCSH: United States. Army--Juvenile literature.
Classification: LCC UA25 .M94 2021 (print) | LCC UA25 (eBook) | DDC 355.1/20973--dc23
LC record available at https://lccn.loc.gov/2020002462
LC eBook record available at https://lccn.loc.gov/2020002463

CONTENTS

AT A GLANCE

- The US Army is the largest branch of the US military. It is also the oldest. It has been defending the country since 1775.

- Soldiers must always be prepared for combat. They undergo tough training. They must stay in peak physical condition.

- More than 1 million people serve in the US Army. The army has about 470,000 active-duty members. About 340,000 people serve in the Army National Guard.

- Most recruits go through Basic Combat Training (BCT). After BCT, the new soldiers begin job training.

- Soldiers who join through the Reserve Officers Training Corps (ROTC) or West Point Military Academy go directly into the army as officers.

- The army offers many career choices, including many that do not involve combat. Soldiers can choose to serve part-time or full-time. Active-duty soldiers work full-time.

- Recruits choose their career path based on their strengths. Their Armed Services Vocational Aptitude Battery (ASVAB) scores show those strength areas.

- There are many army bases in the United States. A base is a camp or another type of army property. Soldiers also serve in other countries.

FIGHTING FIRES

Ryan Earwood was on a mission. So was his crew of firefighters. They worked for the US Army. They needed to put out a fire at the Lawson Army Airfield. This airfield is part of Fort Benning. Fort Benning is an army base in Georgia.

It was December 18, 2019. An airplane was on fire. Fires had broken out on the ground too. The army firefighters tried to

Army firefighters prepare to respond to plane crashes and other types of emergencies where fire is involved.

put out the fires. They worked alongside

firefighters from the Columbus Airport.

The firefighters sprayed water from a

Army firefighters use special equipment to get into buildings that are on fire and collapsing. They practice using this equipment.

water cannon. They aimed at the outside of the plane. Other firefighters ran into the plane.

The inside of the plane was on fire too. The firefighters rushed to put out the flames. Training dummies sat in the plane seats. The firefighters carried them outside to safety.

This was a training exercise. The Fort Benning firefighters do it every year. The airplane is not an actual plane. It is a life-sized model. It does not have wings or wheels. It was made for fire exercises.

Training for combat is an important part of an army soldier's job.

A fire can spread from the outside

to the inside of a plane in just ninety

seconds. Burning jet fuel can reach up

to 1,000 degrees Fahrenheit (538°C).

Special training is required to deal with these fires. Army and airport firefighters learn how to work together. They prepare in case a real emergency happens.

Firefighters play an important role in the US Army. Like other members of the army, they help save lives. Some soldiers serve in combat. Many others, including firefighters, may not. More than 1 million people serve in the army. The army is the largest branch of the US military. Army soldiers risk their lives every day to protect their country.

CHAPTER ONE

HOW DO PEOPLE JOIN THE ARMY?

Army soldiers are always ready to serve. They have honor and courage. They never leave another soldier behind. The US Army looks for people with these traits.

Soldiers in the army have different ranks. Ranks show how much experience soldiers have. High-ranking soldiers are in charge of

Officers develop strategies and lead troops. They must have good problem-solving skills.

many people. They also receive more pay

than lower-ranking soldiers. A staff sergeant

commands eight to sixteen people. A major

general commands up to 16,000 people.

There are three types of army soldiers.

They are enlisted soldiers, officers, and

Teamwork is important in the US Army. Soldiers take care of one another.

warrant officers (WOs). Enlisted soldiers

begin with no military experience. They start

out at the rank of private. This is the lowest

rank in the army. Officers lead enlisted

soldiers. WOs are a special type of enlisted

soldier. They make up less than 3 percent

of the US Army. They have technical skills. Some are engineers. Others work with electronic equipment. They can also organize missions and lead teams. They may train other soldiers.

Army soldiers are part of a team. Everyone has an important job. Major Stephen Wilcox is an officer and a nurse. He says, "It's not about rank or role out here. It's the mission always. We're a team."[1]

ENLISTING

People need to be between the ages of eighteen and thirty-five to join the army. Seventeen-year-olds can join with a parent's permission. The process of joining the army is called enlisting.

Most people begin by talking to a recruiter. Recruiters are experienced soldiers. They give people more information about what it is like to be in the army. They can help people decide if the army is a good fit for them. Many cities and neighborhoods have recruiting offices.

People who decide to enlist are called recruits. A recruit's next step is to take entrance exams. The first exam is the Armed Services Vocational Aptitude Battery (ASVAB) test. It is a multiple-choice test.

Soldiers and recruits can retake the ASVAB. They must wait at least thirty days before retaking the test.

It covers ten subject areas. The subjects include science, math, and reading. The test also covers mechanics, electronics, and **coding**. Recruits need an ASVAB score of at least thirty-one out of ninety-nine to get into the army.

The ASVAB shows what jobs a person might be good at. For example, someone might have a high score in the mechanics section. That person might be good at working with machines. The army uses the ASVAB results to match soldiers with a career.

Recruits also need to take a medical exam. They go to a Military Entrance Processing Station (MEPS). A MEPS doctor makes sure recruits are strong and healthy.

TRAINING

Once they pass these exams, recruits can enlist. They take the oath of enlistment.

Recruits must raise their right hand when they say the oath of enlistment.

This is a promise to protect the United States. Recruits swear they will be loyal to the US Army.

Then recruits go through a special program. It is called reception. Reception can take one to three weeks. Recruits live in barracks. These are buildings that soldiers live in together. Recruits meet their drill sergeants. Drill sergeants give orders. They train recruits.

In reception, recruits meet each other. They get their uniforms. Male recruits get their hair cut short. Many women choose to keep their hair short too. But they can put their hair up instead.

Then recruits take a fitness test. It includes push-ups and sit-ups. Recruits also have to run 1 mile (2 km). Recruits who do not pass this test must get in shape before they move on in the process.

Recruits need to maintain perfect form when they do push-ups.

They work with drill sergeants. The drill sergeants help them get fit.

The next step is Basic Combat Training (BCT). BCT is also known as boot camp. It lasts ten weeks. It challenges recruits physically and mentally. The army has five BCT locations throughout the country.

Drill sergeants oversee recruits throughout BCT. Recruits must obey their commands.

Two of the locations train only men. The

other three train both men and women.

BCT has three phases. The first of these

is the Red Phase. It lasts three weeks.

In this phase, recruits learn to march in

formation. They also learn to think and act like soldiers. They do many fitness drills. They do push-ups and other types of exercises. Drills begin in the Red Phase and continue throughout BCT.

Next is the White Phase. This phase takes another three weeks. Recruits train with weapons. They learn how to use machine guns, hand grenades, and mines. They also learn how to fight without weapons. They go through obstacle courses. They climb towers and swing from ropes. They climb nets and walk across rolling logs.

Recruits learn how to navigate. They develop survival skills. They learn how to give first aid. They also do battle drills. These drills are done in teams. Teams learn how to move an injured soldier to safety.

The final part of BCT is the Blue Phase. It lasts four weeks. Recruits continue doing special drills. They spend several days on a final Field Training Exercise. This exercise tests everything they have learned. Recruits must also pass the Army Physical Fitness Test (APFT). They must do two minutes of sit-ups and two minutes of push-ups. They must also complete a 2-mile

The APFT tests recruits' strength and endurance.

(3-km) timed run. Recruits must meet a minimum standard in each activity to pass. Scoring is based on gender and age. A twenty-five-year-old female recruit needs to do eleven push-ups to pass. She must do forty-three sit-ups. She must complete the run in about twenty minutes.

People who graduate BCT go through a ceremony. Families and friends are invited.

Graduates are given a black hat to wear

with their uniform. This means they are no

longer **civilians**. They are army soldiers.

Sometimes recruits do not do well in

BCT. They may not be physically fit enough.

Or they do not work well in teams. The army

likely will not kick them out. Instead, they go

THE BEST WARRIOR COMPETITION

The US Army holds a special test each year. It is called the Best Warrior Competition. Part of the test involves warrior tasks. These are the same tasks as in BCT. Soldiers also go on a long march. They carry 50 pounds (23 kg) of gear. They have a time limit. They must do all the tasks within this time. The soldier who completes the tasks fastest wins.

back to an earlier phase of BCT to retrain.

The army can dismiss people who still

perform poorly. Then they will be out of the

army. But most recruits make it through.

About 85 percent of recruits graduate BCT.

TYPES OF SERVICE

Some soldiers are active duty. They work

full-time for the army. They serve for two to

six years. People can also join the US Army

Reserve. Reserve soldiers usually have

other jobs. They work part-time for the

army. They commit to three to six years of

service. But they may have to serve longer

in wartime. They train to maintain their skills.

They stay in good physical shape. They may be called on to serve when the army needs them. Then they become active-duty soldiers.

Another option is the Army National Guard. Each state has its own national guard. National guard soldiers serve part-time. They train one weekend a month and two weeks each year. They may be called to serve in an emergency.

OTHER PROGRAMS AND TRAINING

Another way to join the army is through the Reserve Officers Training Corps (ROTC). ROTC is a college training program.

Reserve Officers Training Corps students can compete in a competition called the Ranger Challenge, which includes an obstacle course.

ROTC students go to college for free. The US government pays the cost of their education. ROTC students train to be officers. Those who graduate from ROTC become officers. ROTC graduates do not have to go through BCT.

People can also join the army through West Point Military Academy. This is a four-year college. It is in West Point, New York. It is run by the army. The academy has high standards. To be admitted, students must be recommended by a congressperson or senator. The army pays for students' education and costs of living.

WEST POINT

The West Point site was originally a military fort. It protected American troops during the Revolutionary War (1775–1783). It became a military academy in 1802. Many famous generals graduated from West Point. At first, women were not allowed to attend the school. That did not change until the late 1900s. The first women graduated from West Point in 1980.

It also pays students a **salary**. People who graduate from West Point become officers.

A SOLDIER'S ROLE

What does it mean to be a soldier in the US Army? The best answer comes from the Soldier's Creed. This is a set of beliefs that all soldiers live by. It says that soldiers defend the United States and the American people. They keep their bodies and minds strong. They "never accept defeat" and "never quit."[2] They are always ready for action. And they always put their missions first.

CHAPTER TWO

WHAT TYPES OF JOBS ARE AVAILABLE?

The US Army offers more than 150 different jobs. Soldiers and officers have many options. For example, they can work as engineers and doctors. They can also fly planes and fix machines. Officers supervise or manage other soldiers. They lead military missions too. Each person

Major General Laura Yeager shows soldiers how to use a weapon. Army commanders train soldiers.

plays an important role in supporting

the army.

Army counselors help each recruit

choose a job. They suggest jobs based

on a recruit's ASVAB score. A soldier's

career is called a Military Occupational

Specialty (MOS). Soldiers go to Advanced

Individual Training (AIT) after BCT. AIT is specialized training. Soldiers learn and develop important skills for their job. The length of AIT depends on a soldier's job. For example, a unit supply specialist has eight weeks of AIT. The soldier learns how to

ARMY PILOTS

Josephine and Jared Thompson are married. They are both army pilots. Josephine is a colonel. She helps with medical evacuation (MEDEVAC) missions. MEDEVAC pilots take injured or sick soldiers to safety. Jared tests new aircraft and systems. He is a WO. He says, "We . . . enjoy serving our country while doing what we love to do."

Quoted in Michelle Miller, "Aviation Couple Ascend to Career Milestones," US Army, January 28, 2019. www.army.mil.

ship and store supplies. The supplies may include medicine, food, and **ammunition**. The soldier develops math skills to keep track of these supplies.

ADDITIONAL TRAINING

After AIT, soldiers have on-the-job training. Soldiers often train for their jobs at the same place where they did their BCT. Some train to be infantry soldiers. They learn how to fight on land. Armor soldiers fight in tanks. These soldiers go through BCT and AIT at Fort Benning. Military police and combat engineers train at Fort Leonard Wood. This site is in Missouri. Military police work on army bases. They make sure

everyone follows the army's laws. Some

combat engineers are experts in explosives.

They know how to find hidden bombs.

Sometimes enemies block roads so soldiers

cannot get through. Combat engineers

clear the road. That may mean taking

an obstacle apart or blowing it up. Other

combat engineers build things such as

bridges. They help their team move safely

from one place to another.

Enlisted soldiers who want to become

officers go through additional training. First,

they must have a college degree. Then they

Soldiers go through a special ceremony when they graduate from Officer Candidate School.

go to Officer Candidate School (OCS).

OCS is at Fort Benning. The training lasts

twelve weeks. Civilians or reserve soldiers

with college degrees can also enroll in OCS.

They must complete BCT first. They must

be between the ages of nineteen and

thirty-two years old.

Each army pilot specializes in flying a certain type of aircraft.

Soldiers with technical skills can become WOs. They may be skilled in working with electronics. They use their skills to keep equipment and systems working well. They go to Warrant Officer Candidate School. This school is in Fort Rucker, Alabama.

Some WOs are pilots. They go to Warrant Officer Flight School. This school is also in Fort Rucker.

There are many other specialties in the army too. The army needs different kinds of experts. Each job supports the army.

LAW AND CYBER PROTECTION

There are different groups within the army. One group is the US Army Judge Advocate General's Corps (JAG Corps). This is the army's law firm. Some soldiers work as JAG Corps lawyers. Others work as paralegals. They assist lawyers. JAG Corps lawyers may defend soldiers accused of a crime.

Some argue cases In court. Others teach law classes at military schools.

Another group is the US Army Cyber Command. Not all warfare happens by land, sea, or air. Some of it can happen through computers. The US military stores top-secret information on computers. Enemies may try to break into military computers. Then they could steal this information. The US Army Cyber Command helps protect it. Computer experts help keep army computers secure. They may also attack enemy computers or networks.

The army offers several **cybersecurity** training programs. Some soldiers train at the US Army Cyber School. This school is at Fort Gordon in Georgia. Others go to the Electronic Warfare College. This school is at Fort Sill in Oklahoma.

JOHN FUGH, ARMY LAWYER

John Fugh was born in Beijing, China, in 1934. He came to the United States as a teenager. He trained as a lawyer. Then he joined the US Army. He became the judge advocate general. That's the person who commands the JAG Corps. He was the first Chinese American brigadier general. He later rose to major general. He served in the army for thirty-two years. He received the Distinguished Service Medal. The army gives this award to exceptional leaders.

Soldiers train to become Green Berets at the John F. Kennedy Special Warfare Center and School in North Carolina.

SPECIAL FORCES AND RANGERS

Army soldiers must be in top physical

shape. This is especially true for people

in the US Army Special Forces. These

soldiers are often called the Green Berets.

They work in small teams around the world.

They go on important missions. They fight

terrorists. They rescue captured soldiers.

Sometimes they train other countries'

troops. Green Berets may have special

training in underwater missions. They may

also learn how to parachute from planes.

Some work with bombs. Their jobs are very

dangerous. For this reason, they get extra

training and pay.

Another highly trained force is the

US Army Rangers. The training to become

a Ranger is eight weeks long. Only a

few soldiers are tough enough to pass.

Rangers carry out large **operations**. They

find out where an enemy is hiding. Then

they destroy enemy buildings or supplies.

STUDYING THE ENEMY

Another important army job is human

intelligence collector. Sometimes the

army captures enemies. These people may

have information that would help the army

defeat enemy forces. Human intelligence

collectors try to get the prisoners to share

that information. They cannot use violence

or threats. That would be against the law.

They must understand how people think

and behave. They need to know all about

Army Ranks

Enlisted Soldiers	Warrant Officers	Officers
Private (PVT)	Warrant Officer (WO1)	Second Lieutenant (2LT)
Private Second Class (PV2)	Chief Warrant Officer 2 (CW2)	First Lieutenant (1LT)
Private First Class (PFC)	Chief Warrant Officer 3 (CW3)	Captain (CPT)
Specialist (SPC)	Chief Warrant Officer 4 (CW4)	Major (MAJ)
Corporal (CPL)	Chief Warrant Officer 5 (CW5)	Lieutenant Colonel (LTC)
Sergeant (SGT)		Colonel (COL)
Staff Sergeant (SSG)		Brigadier General (BG)
Sergeant First Class (SFC)		Major General (MG)
Master Sergeant (MSG)		Lieutenant General (LTG)
First Sergeant (1SG)		General (GEN)
Sergeant Major (SGM)		General of the Army (GOA)**
Command Sergeant Major (CSM)		
Sergeant Major of the Army (SMA)*		

* There is only one SMA at a time. The SMA is in charge of all enlisted soldiers.
** A GOA is only appointed in wartime. This has not happened since World War II (1939–1945).

"U.S. Army Ranks," US Army, n.d. www.army.mil.

This chart shows the ranks for different types of soldiers. The lowest ranks are at the top. The highest ranks are at the bottom.

the prisoner's home country. That helps

them gain the prisoner's trust.

Other people study enemy forces.

They come up with ways to fight the enemy.

They are intelligence analysts. They are

good at solving problems. Their skills

are highly valued even outside the army.

Government agencies sometimes hire them.

They may find a job with the Federal Bureau

of Investigation (FBI). The FBI investigates

crimes in the United States. The Central

Intelligence Agency (CIA) may also hire

them. The CIA gathers information about

threats to the country.

OTHER SPECIALIZED JOBS

There are many other specialized jobs in

the army. Some people are information

technology (IT) specialists. They are

computer experts. They know how to fix

Some people are carpentry and masonry specialists. They build things for the army.

computers and computer programs.

The army's computer network is all around

the world. IT specialists are always busy.

Aviation officer is another important job.

Aviation officers fly army helicopters.

They organize and lead flight missions.

Some people work for the Army Medical Readiness Assistance Program. They help soldiers find health care.

They use helicopters to carry troops and supplies. They also strike enemy targets.

CIVILIANS IN THE ARMY

Not everyone who works in the army is a soldier. Sometimes there are more jobs available than there are soldiers. The army can hire civilians for certain jobs.

Civilians can work as nurses or engineers. Others work as scientists or cybersecurity experts. Civilians may work in construction or finance too. These are just a few examples of civilian army jobs.

A WINNING SPIRIT

Members of the army have important roles in defending the country. General James McConville is the army vice chief of staff. He spoke to soldiers at an award ceremony in 2018. He told them, "You didn't come here to try hard. You came here to win. And that's the American spirit—the spirit that we have in the army."[3]

CHAPTER THREE

WHAT IS THE LIFE OF A SOLDIER LIKE?

Each soldier's daily life and routines vary. Soldiers with office jobs might work on base. They have a regular schedule. They get weekends off. But Rangers might be overseas for most of the year. They have many combat missions. Each person's living arrangement is

Infantrymen practice loading and firing weapons as part of their continued training.

different too. Some soldiers live with their

families. Others are not married.

Soldiers are always leading or training

to lead. They know that anything can

Soldiers can train in many parts of the world, such as Germany. This helps them get used to different climates and environments.

happen in combat. Any one of them might

end up leading a team. They must be

ready. Peter J. Schoomaker is a former

army general. He is now retired from the army. He says, "Everybody's got to know how to be a leader."[4]

Soldiers must stay in shape. They exercise regularly. They also must eat healthful foods. They may be deployed at a moment's notice. Deployment happens when the army assigns soldiers to work around the world.

LIFE ON AN ARMY BASE

Active-duty soldiers live on army bases. An army base is like a large neighborhood. Soldiers have everything they may want or need. The Fort Shafter army base in

Honolulu, Hawaii, is one example. It has a

shopping center, gym, and library. It also

has an arts and crafts center and a bowling

alley. Tennis courts and swimming pools are

available to soldiers and their families.

Soldiers can do all their shopping on

the base. They buy groceries at stores

called commissaries. Military exchanges

are another type of store. Soldiers can

buy clothes, furniture, and other items at

these stores. Soldiers get reduced prices

on everything. Bases also have restaurants

where soldiers and their families can eat.

At Fort Carson in Colorado, soldiers can participate in a competition. They march in full gear and are tested on their survival skills.

There are many housing options on army bases. Barracks are one type of housing. Barracks are apartments shared by several people. Recruits usually live in barracks. So do low-ranking soldiers who do not have spouses or children. Higher-ranking soldiers or those who have families have different housing. They live in apartments or houses.

FORT HOOD

Each base has different features. These features depend on who is stationed there. Fort Hood was built in 1942. This army base has two airfields. It can fit 200 aircraft. It also holds 500 tanks and 10,000 vehicles. These vehicles include armored trucks.

Fort Hood is the largest active-duty military base. It is in Kileen, Texas. It covers 340 square miles (880 sq km). About 41,000 soldiers serve at Fort Hood. Nearly 18,000 family members live there.

FAMILY LIFE

The army takes care of soldiers' families. It offers affordable childcare. Soldiers have access to free schools on base. There are playgrounds for children. Many bases also have water parks and indoor pools. Soldiers have affordable health insurance. Their families go to doctors and hospitals on base.

Soldiers who go into ROTC must pass a Combat Water Survival Test. They must swim while carrying a rubber rifle.

Active-duty soldiers have thirty vacation days each year. The army offers many other benefits for families too. Spouses can take college classes on base. The army may give them job opportunities. It also supports families. For example, having a family member deploy can be difficult. Army counselors offer help and support.

EDUCATION

Bases also have education centers. These centers offer soldiers education and leadership training. Counselors help soldiers choose classes. They help soldiers create career goals too.

The army also helps those who want

to continue schooling while enlisted.

Active-duty soldiers and WOs can receive

tuition assistance (TA). TA helps pay for

the costs of college and graduate school.

Soldiers can use their TA at more than

2,000 colleges and universities. They can

BALANCING WORK AND SCHOOL

Sergeant Denys Bulikhov is an active-duty soldier. He was deployed in Afghanistan. He worked on his Master of Science degree during deployment. He was able to balance school and work. He has advice for soldiers who want to earn degrees. He says, "You just have to know that you want it. And continue doing it even [if] it is hard—just like anything else in life."

Quoted in "Sergeant (SGT) Denys Bulikhov," Go Army Ed, 2017. www.goarmyed.com.

study on campus or online. They can learn at their own pace. That means every soldier can set and meet career goals. All soldiers can keep learning. Natisha Baylor is a sergeant in the army. She is a human resource specialist. She helps soldiers with many things, including their finances. She says,

I love the fact that I am helping soldiers. I love the fact that I am making a difference every day. . . . In the army, every day you learn something new.[5]

CHAPTER FOUR

WHAT IS DEPLOYMENT LIKE?

S oldiers move around a lot. Some travel mostly inside the United States. But many live and work in other countries. The army has about 200 bases around the world. More than 1 million people serve in the army. About 470,000 of them are active-duty members.

Some soldiers who are deployed learn how to operate drones. These unmanned flying machines can be used on different types of missions.

In 2019, the US states with the most soldiers were Texas, Georgia, and North Carolina. The army has bases in

Soldiers participate in a training exercise in Hawaii. They learn how to camouflage themselves to hide from or sneak up on enemies.

these states. Among other countries,

Germany had the most US soldiers in 2019.

About 20,000 US soldiers served there.

South Korea was a close second. About

17,000 US troops were stationed there.

Soldiers were also deployed in Saudi Arabia

and many other countries.

DEPLOYMENT

The army switches out teams on a

schedule. When teams deploy, they replace

other teams. Those teams get to go home.

That way, no team is away too long.

One team that deployed in 2019 went

to Afghanistan. This team is known as

the Panther Brigade. Soldiers on this team are paratroopers. They are trained to use parachutes. They parachute into combat situations.

Another team was deployed to Iraq. This team is called the Arctic Wolves. Soldiers on this team drive special combat vehicles. The vehicles are called Strykers. Strykers have eight wheels. There are eighteen different models of Strykers. Many have a cannon on top. They can go up to 60 miles (97 km) per hour. The army has been using Strykers since 2002.

Paratroopers are trained to parachute into enemy territories. They jump out of army aircraft.

A third team was sent to South Korea. This team is known as the Greywolf Brigade. Soldiers on this team trained for a year before deploying. They were in South Korea for nine months. They practiced battle drills with South Korean troops.

IDENTICAL INFANTRYMEN

Joseph and Matthew Maurino are identical twins. They were born less than three minutes apart. They are both in the Army National Guard. They are infantrymen. The brothers deployed together. They were stationed in Qatar in 2019. Qatar is a country in the Persian Gulf. Being together has helped them feel at home. Joseph said, "I haven't felt homesick at all yet."

Quoted in Sergeant Zachary Mott, "Identical Twins Share Deployment Together," US Army Central. June 4, 2019. www.usarcent.army.mil.

Deployment can last from ninety days to fifteen months. Soldiers are usually told about their deployment thirty to ninety days in advance. This gives them and their families time to prepare. Soldiers train for their mission before they are deployed.

Deployment can be hard for soldiers' families. Some soldiers are away for long periods of time. They may miss holidays, birthdays, and other events.

MOVING ABROAD

Soldiers often come back home when their mission ends. Families may stay home and wait for them to return. But sometimes soldiers move to a new country. Their families may move with them.

Moving can be an adventure. But it can also be stressful. The country's culture or customs may be strange. Soldiers and their families might have to learn a new language. The money may be different. The food may be unfamiliar. Adjusting to these changes takes time. Soldiers and families may feel homesick. It helps when family and friends back home keep in touch.

The army offers a Relocation Readiness Program (RAP). RAP helps soldiers and their families settle into their new homes.

Soldiers who are deployed may not see their families for a long time. The army arranges welcome-home ceremonies when they return.

It provides counseling. It helps them adjust to their new lives.

The army may not tell people where their family member was deployed. It may do this when a soldier is on a secret mission. Secrecy helps keep them safe. The army

KEEPING SECRETS

Soldiers need to be careful when they talk to their families. They cannot share details about a mission. They cannot explain where or how troops are moving. Speaking about problems with a mission is also off-limits. Soldiers could be in danger if these details get out. Enemies could learn of the army's plans. Missions could fail.

does not want this information to get out. But soldiers can still communicate with their families. Army bases have phones and internet access. Soldiers can also write letters and send mail.

Army soldiers live and work in many countries. Wherever they are, they must always stay true to the army's values. They serve the United States. They protect Americans all over the world. John Antal is a retired army colonel. He wrote, "As long as there is an army, there will be an America."[6]

GLOSSARY

ammunition

objects such as bullets that are fired from weapons

civilian

someone who is not in the military

coding

writing commands that tell computers what to do

cybersecurity

actions taken to protect computers and computer networks from an attack

formation

a certain order or arrangement in which soldiers gather

intelligence

important or secret information about enemy forces

operations

actions done by the military, such as attacks or raids

salary

a fixed payment that someone receives regularly for doing a certain job

terrorists

people who target and attack certain people or groups

CHAPTER ONE: HOW DO PEOPLE JOIN THE ARMY?

1. Terry Goodman, "Army Medical-Civilian Trauma Team Supports Field Training Exercise on Joint Base Lewis-McChord," *US Army*, December 17, 2019. www.army.mil.

2. "Army Values: Soldier's Creed," *US Army*, n.d. www.army.mil.

CHAPTER TWO: WHAT TYPES OF JOBS ARE AVAILABLE?

3. Joe Lacdan, "Winners of Best Warrior Contest Announced, Earn NCO, Soldier of the Year Titles," *US Army*, October 10, 2018. www.army.mil.

CHAPTER THREE: WHAT IS THE LIFE OF A SOLDIER LIKE?

4. *The Soldier's Guide*. New York: Skyhorse Publishing, 2016, 6–8.

5. "Road To Becoming a 42 Alpha, Human Resources Specialist," *GoArmy*, May 3, 2016. www.youtube.com/watch?v=tAU1zXCh7eE.

CHAPTER FOUR: WHAT IS DEPLOYMENT LIKE?

6. Robert F. Dorr, *Alpha Bravo Delta Guide to the U.S. Army*. New York: Hudson Books, 2003, vi.

FOR FURTHER RESEARCH

BOOKS

Roberta Baxter, *Work in the Military*. San Diego, CA: ReferencePoint Press, 2020.

Peter Kohl, *My Dad Is in the Army*. New York: PowerKids Press, 2016.

Julian Lowe, *My Aunt Is in the Army Reserve*. New York: PowerKids Press, 2016.

Lee Slater, *Army Rangers*. Minneapolis, MN: Abdo Publishing, 2016.

Michael V. Uschan, *Careers in the US Army*. San Diego, CA: ReferencePoint Press, 2016.

INTERNET SOURCES

"Army Workout Plan," *US Army*, October 12, 2018. www.goarmy.com.

"Military Careers," *US Bureau of Labor Statistics*, September 19, 2019. www.bls.gov/ooh/military.

"Service Branches: Army," *Today's Military*, 2020. www.todaysmilitary.com.